Read and Rhyme
LEVEL 3 ★★★

A Snack for Zack

by Spencer Brinker

Consultant:
Beth Gambro
Reading Specialist
Yorkville, Illinois

Contents

BEARPORT
PUBLISHING

New York, New York

A Snack for Zack

This is **Jack**.

This is **Jack**'s pet duck **Zack**.

Jack carries **Zack** in a **pack** on his **back**.

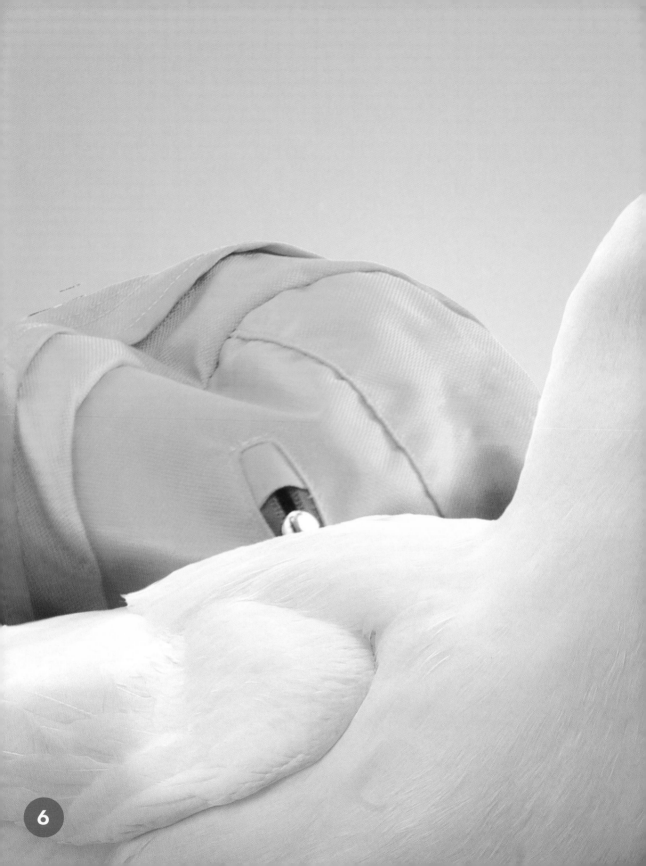

Quack! Quack! Zack wants a **snack**.

Jack sees a little **black shack.**

Inside the **shack** is a big **snack rack**.

Zack flies out of the **pack**.

Jack yells, "Come **back**!"

Jack grabs **Zack**,
who's eating his **snack**.

Yum! Yum!
Quack! Quack!

Key Words in the -ack Family

back

black

pack

quack

rack   **shack**   **snack**

Other **-ack** Words: **attack, crack, lack, sack**

Index

About the Author

Spencer Brinker loves to tell "dad jokes" and play word games with his twin girls.

Teaching Tips

Before Reading

✔ Introduce rhyming words and the **–ack** word family to readers.

✔ Guide readers on a "picture walk" through the text by asking them to name the things shown.

✔ Discuss book structure by showing children where text will appear consistently on pages. Highlight the supportive pattern of the book.

During Reading

✔ Encourage readers to "read with your finger" and point to each word as it is read. Stop periodically to ask children to point to a specific word in the text.

✔ Reading strategies: When encountering unknown words, prompt readers with encouraging cues such as:

- **Does that word look like a word you already know?**
- **Does it rhyme with another word you have already read?**

After Reading

✔ Write the key words on index cards.

- **Have readers match them to pictures in the book.**

✔ Ask readers to identify their favorite page in the book. Have them read that page aloud.

✔ Choose an **–ack** word. Ask children to pick a word that rhymes with it.

✔ Ask children to create their own rhymes using **–ack** words. Encourage them to use the same pattern found in the book.

Credits: Cover, © photomaster/Shutterstock, © JpegPhotographer/Shutterstock, © hsagencia/Shutterstock, and © Jiang Hongyan/Shutterstock; 2, © Cherry-Merry/Shutterstock; 3, © photomaster/Shutterstock and © Photographee.eu/Shutterstock; 4–5, © Cherry-Merry/Shutterstock and © photomaster/Shutterstock; 6–7, © photomaster/Shutterstock and © Cherry-Merry/Shutterstock; 8–9, © FridaV/Shutterstock and © doomu/Shutterstock; 10–11, © B. Forenius/Shutterstock, © Denis Semenchenko/Shutterstock, © Robyn Mackenzie/Shutterstock, © Jiang Zhongyan/Shutterstock, © Jiang Hongyan/Shutterstock, © Chones/Shutterstock, and © motorolka/Shutterstock; 12, © Pixels-Dot/Shutterstock; 13, © Cherry-Merry/Shutterstock; 14–15, © Cherry-Merry/Shutterstock, © photomaster/Shutterstock, © motorolka/Shutterstock, and © Jiang Zhongyan/Shutterstock; 16T (L to R), © Fuller Photography/Shutterstock, © Cherry-Merry/Shutterstock, and © photomaster/Shutterstock; 16B (Lto R), © Denis Semenchenko/Shutterstock, © FridaV/Shutterstock, and © Yulia Sverdlova/Shutterstock.

Publisher: Kenn Goin   **Senior Editor**: Joyce Tavolacci   **Creative Director**: Spencer Brinker

Library of Congress Cataloging-in-Publication Data: Names: Brinker, Spencer, author. | Gambro, Beth, consultant. Title: A snack for Zack / by Spencer Brinker; consultant: Beth Gambro, Reading Specialist, Yorkville, Illinois. Description: New York, New York : Bearport Publishing, [2020] | Series: Read and rhyme: Level 3 | Includes index. Identifiers: LCCN 2019007134 (print) | LCCN 2019012634 (ebook) | ISBN 9781642806151 (Ebook) | ISBN 9781642805611 (library) | ISBN 9781642807240 (pbk.) Subjects: LCSH: Readers (Primary) Classification: LCC PE1119 (ebook) | LCC PE1119 .B751875 2020 (print) | DDC 428.6—dc23 LC record available at https://lccn.loc.gov/2019007134

10 9 8 7 6 5 4 3 2 1